A PERILOUS M

The Story of Grace Darling

Norman Sneesby

Isle House

ISBN No. 0–9551031–0–X

Production by Chapman & Harvey Ltd. Ely 01353 661524

ACKNOWLEDGEMENTS

Front Cover: Royal National Lifeboat Institution.

Frontispiece: Northumberland Record Office. Reproduced with the permission of Ward Philipson Group Ltd.

Pages 18,21(left), 33(top): Royal National Lifeboat Institution

Pages 19 (right), 20, 21 (right): National Portrait Gallery

Pages 19 (left), 31: Northumberland Record Office

Pages 28, 29 (author's photographs): The Corporation of Trinity House

Page 34: The National Maritime Museum, Greenwich

All other photographs were taken by the author.

Maps reproduced by permission of Ordnance Survey on behalf of HMSO. © Crown Copyright 2005. All rights reserved. Ordnance Survey Licence Number SAP 48685.

The primary sources of the quotations from William, Grace and Thomasin Darling are 1) "Grace Darling: her True Story. From unpublished papers in possession of her family" by Thomasin Darling 1880. 2) "Grace Darling and her Times" by Constance Smedley 1932. "Grace had an English Heart" by Jessica Mitford 1988 includes informative graphics.

Grace Horsley Darling
born 24 November 1815
died 20 October 1842

For our grandchildren Amie, Josh,
Ben and Daniel, George and Eleanor

Author's Note

I confess that I do not belong to Northumberland, though I have visited that delightful county many times. I am an East Anglian, and although I have seen at first hand and on numerous occasions the terribly destructive power of the North Sea, I cannot claim descent from the historic county wherein the heroine and her equally heroic father were born and bred.

But the Darlings, while they are forever Northumberland, belong also to the rest of our country, and are also known to some people across the seas.

In my first few paragraphs I have tried to set out the reasons why I have taken the liberty of writing about the family history, the legendary rescue, and the sad aftermath, and I can only hope true Northumbrians will be indulgent towards my efforts to tell this uplifting story.

Most grateful thanks to my wife Pat for her advice and unfailing patience, to Rodney Dale for some valuable comments, and to family and friends who helped me during my continuing struggles with the computer.

Norman Sneesby

CONTENTS

	Page
Remembrances	11
The Darlings as Lightkeepers	13
Grace Darling's Birthplace	14
Grace's Mother and Father	16
An Image of Grace Darling	19
Brownsman Island	23
Moving to the Longstone	25
The Rescue	27
The Aftermath	35
"She Went like Snow"	38

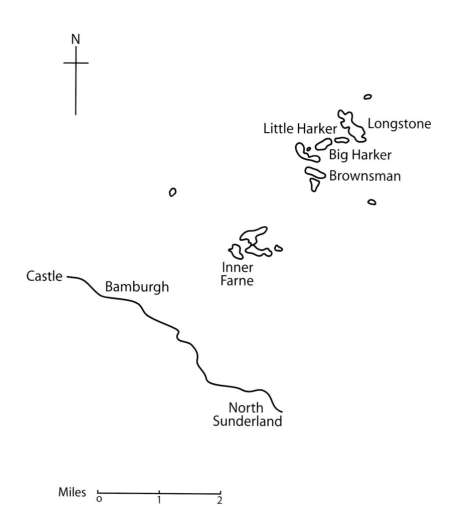

N

Longstone

Little Harker

Big Harker

Brownsman

Castle

Bamburgh

Inner
Farne

North
Sunderland

Miles
0   1   2

*Location map of the Farne Islands as they appear at low water, showing those
referred to in the story. At high tide some parts are submerged.*

A PERILOUS MISSION

The Story of Grace Darling

This is the story of something very courageous that happened a long time ago. It is so remarkable as to be hard to believe, yet we know it is one-hundred percent true. It tells of a fifty-four-year-old father and his daughter of twenty-two rowing out in an open boat for over a mile in fearsome seas and a howling gale, to reach a bare windswept rock and to rescue nine survivors of the wreck of a large steamship.

Remembrances

When I was a child, before the last war, the narrative of Grace Darling was everywhere. My own childhood books made much of the story of this exceptionally brave young woman, and she became the heroine of thousands, if not millions, of children throughout the country. As a boy my own heroes were cricketers, speedway riders and intrepid explorers for the most part, but I did have one special heroine, and she was Grace Darling. I have in front of me an account written in the thirties, and typical of many in childrens' encyclopaedias at that time. And of course there were many story-books about Grace Darling. There are still a few, but now things are rather different. More than 170 years after the event much has intervened to overtake the story, so that today she is less talked about, and may even be unknown, outside her own part of the country. But she has always been the particular heroine of the brave lifeboat men and women, and in 1938 the Royal National Lifeboat Institution built a museum to her memory on land given by the owners of the great castle which overlooks Grace's own village of Bamburgh in Northumberland.

Thousands, young and old, visit this museum, but the collection has been very cramped, and the RNLI have planned to increase the size of the museum and to provide a new educational facility; this imaginative project will much enhance the appeal to all ages.

I had been to the museum once before, but not so long ago my wife and I spent some days in this beautiful part of the world and we revisited the small room – for it was no more than that – to see once more the Grace Darling memorabilia. In superb weather we were able to take two journeys around the Farne Islands off the Northumbrian coast, and when we landed on one of these National Trust reserves we could walk among puffins and come very close to the cliff-top nests of the shags. The trip was about twelve miles long including the various diversions, and it included the actual route of the famous rescue. It was on the Inner Farne that we were able to land and see the birds.

But most evocative to me was landing on a forbidding slab of bare rock called Longstone Island, entering the lighthouse and climbing one hundred steps to the top, and looking out on exactly what Grace would have seen when she first spied the wreck of the paddle-steamer. Close by me were learned explanations of the automatic mechanism of the lantern, but we had just twenty minutes inside the lighthouse and I can only say that I was more interested in recalling the story of Grace Darling.

It must have been at this time, and during our sea journey which retraced the rescue route of Grace and her father in their rowing-boat, that I realised that the heroine of my childhood remained that same heroine in my ripe old age, and that I would like to make some contribution, however small, to keeping her memory alive. That is why I have written this short story.

I have now come to believe that my grandmother, who was born a few years after Grace died, was named after her. I can detect no-one else called Grace in the family ancestry, so I cannot but think that my grandmother, the first-born of the family, was named after her parents' childhood heroine. I can readily imagine that this is true. And Grace Darling's signature, careful and painstaking, is in the same immaculate copperplate as that of my own Grace, whose writings I still possess.

So here is the story, with its legendary deed of rescue. It is at once absorbing, moving and inspiring, and I hope I can do justice to it.

THE DARLINGS AS LIGHTKEEPERS

In the mid-eighteenth century a Scotsman named Robert Darling walked the lanes from his town of Duns to the village of Belford in Northumberland. This young Scotsman came to be Grace Darling's grandfather. Belford was a busy stopping-point on the Great North Road, and its taverns did a rousing trade, so that once Robert had trained to be a cooper – a maker of casks, kegs and barrels – he was never short of work. In Belford he met Elizabeth Clarke, and they were married in 1769. They had seven children, of whom five died young – a not uncommon fate in those days. But the last child was a singularly healthy boy; he was born in 1786 and christened William, and he became Grace's father.

It was several years later that William's own father was appointed keeper of a new lighthouse on Brownsman Island, one of the islands called the Farnes. Why they were given this name no-one knows, but it comes from an old-English word meaning "fern", so it may be that some of the islands had a growth of ferns, but now even the habitable ones have only a dusty soil, with rabbit-holes, puffin-burrows, grass and nettles. The islands are mostly bare rock, much submerged, with only a few projections above the highest tide. They consist of a material called dolerite, said to be the hardest rock in the world, and one can imagine how terribly dangerous the sea can be anywhere close by, and why some sort of light has always been essential to guide shipping.

The first lighthouse was located on the Inner Farne, to direct ships into a relatively sheltered channel, called the Fairway, between this island and the mainland. Today's lighthouse is "state of the art", but in the early days it would have been no more than a thirty-foot square tower. There are several of these so-called "peel-towers", which date back to Tudor times when they were fortified dwelling-places. Only later did they become light-towers, with braziers burning coal throughout the night. Ladders were attached to the walls, and the lightkeeper and his assistant had to climb these vertical ladders with loads of coal on their backs – not a job for the faint-hearted or the sufferer from vertigo.

Another of these ancient towers was located on Brownsman Island, which is in the chain known as the Outer Farnes, and in 1795 the Scotsman William Darling was appointed keeper of this very basic light-tower. No-one knows how or why he got this job, since he had no previous experience; perhaps he was the only person ready and willing to climb the precarious ladder, but it may be that his well-connected wife played a helpful part. Anyway, he seems to have made a good job of it. William went with him and the family lived in a stone cottage built under the wall of the tower. However William decided early on to become the boatman between Bamburgh village and the light-tower, and to lodge in the village. William always chafed at being subordinate to anyone; he was a natural leader and made no bones about it.

GRACE DARLING'S BIRTHPLACE

The village of Bamburgh is sheltered from the pounding North Sea by high dunes and dominated by the great castle once owned by Lord Crewe, Bishop of Durham. The village became a kind of protectorate of the castle, and the people were well looked after. A free school and a library were installed within the castle, while the sick of the village, together with shipwrecked mariners, were cared for. Food was sold cheaply, so that no-one ever went hungry. By the standards of the time Bamburgh was a good place in which to live, with plenty of employment on the estates belonging to Lord Crewe's Trustees.

The great castle, whose ancestry goes back to Saxon times, is built above a huge crag of very hard rock, which has proved insurmountable over the centuries. The line of rocks continues seawards to form the Farne islands

The village of Bamburgh

It was in a house on the landward outskirts of the village, and adjoining a large walled orchard, that William Darling had his lodgings. The orchard belonged to the castle, and William's elderly landlord, Job Horsley, was its caretaker. Job and Grace Horsley, both from Northumbrian farming stock, had a daughter named – rather strangely to our ears – Thomasin. Thomasin, submissive by nature and living a sheltered life, exhibited throughout her days a decided aversion to the sea, but nevertheless in 1805 she and William were married, when he was nineteen and she was thirty-one.

William's father was still lightkeeper on Brownsman island, but much had changed. Perhaps the venerable Robert Darling had been born under a lucky star, for in 1810 the historic but ineffective tower was replaced by a purpose-built oil-fired lighthouse. The lucky star quickly faded, however, for Robert and his wife were not long to enjoy their new workplace. By 1815 – the year of Grace's birth – both had died, and William the son had taken over the new lighthouse. William already had six children, and his seventh – Grace Horsley Darling – was born on 24th November 1815; she was named after her maternal grandmother who had died two months earlier. Grace's mother Thomasin had come into her parents' house in Bamburgh for the birth of this seventh child; it seems there were no problems, and Grace was a healthy baby. There were now four girls, and the coming of twin boys would ultimately bring the family to nine.

The house where Grace Darling was born

The small house, at the end of Bamburgh village, still stands, across the road from St Aidan's church, and the museum adjoins it. A plaque above the door records Grace's birth and its date.

And now, with our stage entirely occupied by the Darling family,
It is time to take a look at them.

GRACE'S MOTHER AND FATHER

We will start with the least significant figure – at least in this narrative – Grace's mother Thomasin. She was forty-one when Grace was born, and she subsequently had the twin boys. At the time of the epic rescue she would have been sixty-three. One of a very few depictions shows her of indeterminate age, quite stoutly built, with a careworn countenance. She has been virtually ignored by the story-tellers, but she rose to the occasion on that one fateful morning, and indeed without her contribution no rescue would have been possible.

Mrs Darling was thoroughly domesticated and saw her job, in an environment totally alien to her upbringing, as looking after her large family and not concerning herself with other matters. Some have said she could neither read nor write, but she could care for her children, make and mend their clothes, and keep them fit on her legendary rabbit-pies. She was also very good at making eider-downs from the down collected from the nests of the eider-ducks once the young birds had left.

We have no illustrations of her children other than Grace, apart from a very fuzzy photograph of an older daughter, also called Thomasin, and one of William Brooks, one of the twin boys. When the twins were born the Darlings' eldest child was only thirteen, so there would have been eleven in the household to be fed and clothed. We should therefore have the greatest respect for Mrs Darling.

One by one the children, as they grew up, left home, with various outcomes. Two of the boys ultimately became lighthouse-keepers themselves, and the others found themselves doing skilled work on the mainland. Three of the older girls married locally, and only Thomasin remained single. Two of these three girls died fairly young, one thirty-five and the other thirty-two. One son died at twenty, possibly killed in an accident. Grace was now thirteen, and his loss must have affected her greatly at the time.

At the head of this large household was their father William Darling.

There are good likenesses of William Darling. He was tall and upright, and had done some army training as a young man. He had a smallish mouth and a well-developed chin, and these features were passed on to Grace.

William Darling was a man of stature in every way. He was always in command of a situation, and his bravery is thoroughly documented. With two of his sons he succeeded in rescuing three crewmen of a small boat wrecked on the Longstone rocks; this was a truly courageous rescue in appalling conditions. Grace was still young at the time, and this must have reinforced her abiding respect, amounting almost to reverence, for her father. To Grace Mr Darling was an infallible guide and mentor, and very much in charge of the family.

He was, moreover, a man of many parts. He was a great reader and a frequent visitor to the castle's free library. He was also an excellent teacher, and his children benefited from their lessons in history and geography. There is no doubt that he was a highly religious man, and Grace wrote later that most of her books were tracts and sermons; her father had no time at all for novels. His regime was therefore a restrictive one, and some of the family may not have been entirely sorry to seek occupation elsewhere. But not Grace, who in her undemanding way followed her father's lead in so many ways.

William Darling, 1786 –1865

The parental influence on the family, and especially on Grace, can be seen in one of her letters:

"I have been brought up on the islands, learned to read and write by my parents, and knit, sew and spin; indeed I have no time to spare, but when I have been on the Main I am quite surprised to see people generally after what they call getting their day's work done, they sit down, some to play at cards, which I do not understand, perhaps as well, for my father says they are some of the Devil's books; others to read romances, novels and plays, which are books my father will not allow a place in our house, for he says they are throwing away time."

AN IMAGE OF GRACE DARLING

What of Grace Darling herself? During her period of fame she was drawn and painted many times by impecunious artists, and even sculpted. At one time there was an army of nine painters in the lighthouse, and her father had to limit their numbers. Inevitably the portraits are by no means alike. Some were Grace's own preference; others were more acceptable to different members of her family.

An often reproduced portrait, showing the "Grace Darling hat"

Grace's own favourite picture, which she agreed to autograph

19

The portrait with the hat, a creation of beaver and satin presented by the hatters of Berwick-upon-Tweed, and worn by Grace in acknowledgement of their generosity, has a rather expressionless countenance, reflecting little if anything of Grace's personality. But is is almost certainly the best-known picture of Grace Darling, having been reproduced so many times.

The second painting was done by Henry Perlee Parker, who became a close friend of the family. There is some carping at the depiction of Grace in clothing unsuited to lighthouse living, but Grace did like to dress up a bit. A less trivial opinion is that the face has a sad, or at least wistful, expression. Those with this view should take another look and observe the firm-set mouth and lively, confident eyes in this very good portrait. It is no wonder that Grace liked it and was happy to sign it.

Grace Darling's signature

A Victorian lady called Eva Hope wrote a very long and rambling account of Grace Darling and the famous rescue. There are many inaccuracies, and the book is filled with the sentiment beloved in those times, but the description of Grace's build and features bears the stamp of accuracy, and is confirmed in other writings. "Grace was rather beneath the ordinary stature, and her figure was slender and graceful. She had a wreath of sunny brown curls, and a delicate clear complexion, which revealed the quick emotions of joy or sorrow that moved her." Putting on one side the sentimental language, there is no doubt that she was slight and less than robust, and this makes her performance during the rescue even more remarkable.

The essential Grace Darling seemed impossible to capture in a single painting, but the most talented of the artists was Perlee Parker, and his portraits are very evocative. He must have had some empathy with Grace, because they got on very well. He has two other pictures shown here. The completed one only came to light in the 1960s, and its appearance is calm and peaceful. The other is little more than an outline, purposely left uncompleted; its delicacy is there for all to see, and the portrait seems to be showing us something of the true personality of the artist's subject.

Two portraits by Perlee Parker

During her brief period of fame there were many writings about her appearance. Thus her far-seeing eyes were considered as becoming a person on a remote lighthouse, and without doubt Grace was used to scanning the horizons by day and by night.

A hoard of money-grabbers left behind them a very mixed bag of crudities, including bogus locks of hair. (Indeed it is reported that Grace's brother William Brooks was so infuriated by these that he kicked one brazen offender out of the door.) But as far as paintings and lithographs were concerned the family seemed to be looking for an illustration of a true lighthouse daughter, perhaps wearing the very shawl she had thrown over her shoulders for the rescue. This was "our Gracie", direct and unsophisticated, the person they knew every day of their lives.

What emerges from all these pictures and written descriptions is a serious, self-reliant young woman, naturally shy with strangers but always making a great effort to be polite and affable to them. She was highly companionable within her own family, and in no sense reclusive. She had a strong set of beliefs instilled into her by her father, and also inherited from him the desire to make a good job of everything she did, whether it was in perfecting her handwriting or in observing carefully and writing down the habits of the many varieties of seabirds that she saw and associated with every day. She was a very responsible person, and could safely be relied on to look after the lamp at the top of the lighthouse. She worked hard at keeping the rooms and stairways clean, perhaps musing meanwhile on all the knowledge instilled into her during her family lessons, and never seemed to complain. And she became adept at handling an oar in the fishing-boat called a coble, on expeditions with her father.

Despite the limitations on her way of life Grace never, as far as we know, showed a desire to broaden her horizons. It was her duty as well as her pleasure to be a responsible helper in her lighthouse, and indeed the very word to sum her up would be "dutiful". Her father was the respected captain of his lighthouse-ship, and Grace saw herself as a worthy member of his crew.

The sign outside the Museum at Bamburgh

BROWNSMAN ISLAND

For the first ten years of her life Grace lived in the cottage on Brownsman island. On one side was the disused tower, and on the other the forty-three-foot lighthouse; this has only recently been dismantled to repair and restore the house, which is used by wardens of the National Trust in the summer months. From the shore it is not always possible to distinguish Brownsman island, where this early lighthouse was sited.

On this misty morning it is not possible to see the Longstone lighthouse five miles away, but the structures on the nearer island of Brownsman are just discernible.

Not long after the construction of this lighthouse it was evident that the positioning was wrong and that it was not tall enough, so the decision was made to decommission it and build a new one on Longstone island; this is considerably further out and the last island to have some parts showing above water when the tide is full. So in 1825 a team of workmen carried out the laborious and often dangerous task of building this new lighthouse. A so-called "barracks" was put up to house them – in the course of time this was buffeted to pieces by the towering waves – and sometimes they had to be roped together for safety, but the lighthouse, a beautiful structure eighty-five feet high, was duly completed, and the family moved into their new quarters.

The surroundings of the Longstone lighthouse were very different from those on Brownsman island. The Brownsman remained almost entirely above water at high tide, and was covered with a thin but nutritious soil, with a wide variety of bird life and a thriving population of rabbits who, if they were lucky, avoided Mr Darling's gun and Mrs Darling's famous pies. William Darling, industrious as ever, had built a wall to keep both rabbits and wind away, and he had created a small garden outside the cottage where he could grow some basic vegetables, some rhubarb, and any other plant that could survive the gales. Nevertheless sometimes his garden was devastated by strong winds and the whole process had to be undertaken afresh.

Life on the Brownsman had indeed been a pleasant one, and sometimes in the summer not only relations appeared, but also naturalists to do some bird-watching, some having to be accommodated within the cottage. The visitors were welcome for the money they brought in – for some expensive provisions had to be purchased on the mainland – and they may well have been regaled by the stories of Mr Darling. He played the violin and had a good singing voice with which he treated his children to old Northumbrian songs, and perhaps he entertained his guests in this manner. Grace undoubtedly enjoyed her childhood days on Brownsman island, where she could play with the twin boys and make pets out of some of the tamest birds, especially the eider-ducks.

The house on Brownsman island.

A few words about the eider-ducks. They lay their eggs on the ground, and pluck their own down to keep the eggs warm, because their natural home is in arctic regions. When approached they remain on their nests through thick and thin, and so Grace could go and seemingly make friends with them. Later the down would be collected and cleaned, and Mrs Darling would set to and make bed-covers and linings for clothes.

MOVING TO THE LONGSTONE

But at the age of ten Grace's way of life changed abruptly, for the Longstone was a far harder environment.

Longstone island lies about a mile beyond the Brownsman. I have walked on this island, which is no more than a flat slippery sheet of very hard rock, mostly covered at high tide, but showing a little strand at low water. It is one of the most forbidding places I can ever remember visiting. There is little or no wild life, for birds have nowhere to nest, though Mr Darling, an enthusiastic naturalist, took great pains to move some sand to form a shelf above tide level and provide an environment for them as best he could. All that has long since gone, and we are left with this stark slab of unyielding black stone, washed incessantly by the swell and by the fearsomely high waves which are so common in the seas along this coast.

This outcrop of jagged rock is virtually devoid of wildlife, and the surface is dangerously slippery at all times

The Longstone lighthouse

This is indeed a grim place on which to be living in a lonely lighthouse, itself not immune to being wave-washed in the crashing storms. After the pleasures of the Brownsman life must have been something of a tread-mill, and now there were only four left in the lighthouse: the father and mother, Grace and one of the twin boys, William Brooks, who was being groomed to take over from his father. Everyone else had departed to the mainland. Yet Grace continued without demur to do her maintenance work. In fact she seemed to take pleasure in the knowledge that she was doing her job, and made every effort to do it well, knowing she was invaluable to her father. She certainly spent a lot of time sewing and clothes-making, and there were books to read, albeit of very limited range.

But Grace would have taken the greatest pleasure in going out with her father on a smooth day to do some fishing, for these waters teem with fish, and Grace seemed to have a real empathy with the sea, and was well capable of plying an oar.

On a calm day Grace would go out with her father and brothers, through this stretch of sea, to tend the crops on Brownsman island, where William Darling retained permission to grow what he could.

26

Despite the drawbacks Grace was perhaps able to spread her wings a bit, for it was said that during her middle years she attended a school at Spittal, near Berwick-upon-Tweed, the school being run by the mother of a friend. There is no record of Grace confirming this, and while Mr Darling's terse journal gives it no mention he was always anxious to get his daughter out and about, and he would have welcomed the chance to further her accomplishments. Whatever the truth, and whether she stayed as a pupil or a helper, Grace learned to put together excellent English, though she was never a good speller. She was a prolific letter-writer; her words are lively and positive and provide a remarkable insight into her feelings and attitudes throughout her life.

The lighthouse of today was damaged by a bomb during the war but restored, and both inside and out its basic form is much as it was in the time of the Darlings. However a number of modern ancillary structures have been erected on the rock below, so that the overall appearance is somewhat changed.

In the time of the Darlings the lowest room was the living-room and kitchen, and the upper sections were bedrooms, with beds built into the walls. Grace's room was the uppermost one, just below the storage compartment and the lantern itself. There are one hundred steps, mainly of stone, spiralling up to the top, and I can vouch for their steepness.

And so we come to the remarkable – almost unbelievable – story of that historic episode ending in the great moment of rescue.

THE RESCUE

From the top of the lighthouse can be seen at low water a shapeless bare rock called the Big Harker. Adjoining it is the Little Harker, and closer to the lighthouse are the Blue Caps, largely under water at high tide.

That is what Grace would have seen on a calm clear day. But on the night of the 7th of September 1838 it was a very different story. During the preceding evening there had been every sign that an exceptional storm was brewing up. Brooks the son, who spent quite long periods with his fishermen friends on the mainland, had been over there for some time, and there was no chance of his returning in such conditions, so only Grace and her parents were left in the lighthouse.

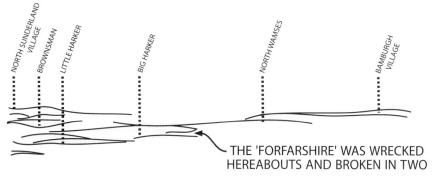

THE 'FORFARSHIRE' WAS WRECKED
HEREABOUTS AND BROKEN IN TWO

Grace's view from the lighthouse in fine weather

It was after midnight when everything had been brought in and stowed away, the boat had been securely lashed, and after carrying out his check on the lantern Grace's father went to bed and fell asleep.

Grace was awake before dawn, and it is sometimes written that she then looked through the small window by her room. If so she could have seen little or nothing through the streaming window, and in the murky light. More probably, as the unofficial assistant light-keeper, she mounted the steep wooden stairway leading from her room to the lantern.

In the morning of the rescue Grace climbed these wooden steps to the lantern.

It would have been a quarter of an hour before dawn as Grace prepared to extinguish the light, but now, from the outside balcony, she seemed to discern a huge vessel, broken in two, some three-quarters of a mile away at the far end of the Big Harker reef. Overhead was heavy cloud, and below was a crashing sea throwing spray over most of the Big Harker; there appeared a white mist over everything, and it was impossible in the half-light to make out what had happened.

The precise details of how the ship ran on to the rock are not the concern of this narrative. The up-to-date steamship "Forfarshire" had been bound from Hull to Dundee, carrying both passengers and crew. This fine vessel was halfway to Dundee on this inaugural voyage when one of the boilers sprang a leak, and the remaining one could not operate. As the wind swung north the vessel was helpless; she was swept southward and was ultimately dashed against the Big Harker. The ship broke in two and some forty-six people, including almost all the passengers, were immediately washed away and drowned.

So what met Grace's eyes was the terrifying image of half this large ship, with her broken paddles, imprisoned on the jagged rock three-quarters of a mile away. It was still only half-light, and impossible to make out any detail. Grace rushed down to wake her father, and together they scanned the wreck through the large telescope to see if there was any sign of life. There seemed to be none. The conditions remained dreadful, but, as William Darling reported "the glass was incessantly applied", and as daylight emerged they could pick out three or four figures on the lee side of the rock.

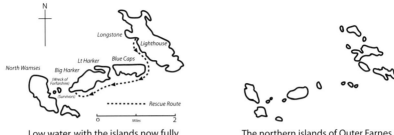

Low water, with the islands now fully
exposed, showing the route of the rescue

The northern islands of Outer Farnes at
high tide, with parts now submerged

The distant islands of the Outer Farnes on the 7th of September 1838.
© *Crown Copyright. All rights reserved. Licence Number SAP48685*

Grace was now beside herself with anxiety, and in a state of emotion so unlike her usual calm self she was virtually screaming through the wild storm to her father: we must go in the boat to save these people.

But let Grace herself, writing later, tell the story:

"I had little thought of anything but to exert myself to the utmost, my spirit was worked up by the sight of such a dreadful affair that I can imagine I still see the sea flying over the vessel".

And again:

"...though not without a feeling of sorrow that we were not enabled to do more but the Almighty who preserved us throughout had ordered otherwise, for not one minute was lost on discerning three persons alive".

William Darling was a brave man – none braver – but he did not see how a boat needing three men in rough weather could possibly reach the island through the mountainous seas. His daughter was lightly built and not very robust. But he thought quickly: the tide is falling, and if we can by any means reach the reef there may be crewmen there to help row back to the lighthouse "without which we could not return". Mr Darling said later that Grace declared "that if he declined to accompany her, she would go alone, and that, live or die, she would make the attempt to save them". This would of course have been impossible. But the decision had to be William Darling's, though his subsequent report does say that "we agreed" about the return with the crewmen. Grace herself put it this way:

30

"It was sufficient to affect the strongest nerve to view the wreck. I was very anxious, and did render every assistance that lay within my power, but my father was equally so, and needed not to be urged by me, being experienced in such things, and knowing what could be done".

William Darling managed to quieten his daughter, and they threw on their warmest clothes. Grace put her plaid shawl around her shoulders, and blankets and additional oars were piled into the boat. But now there came the problem of bringing the coble from the open boathouse and launching her into the small haven by the lighthouse wall.

Cobles in Amble harbour, Northumberland. William Darling's coble was sturdily built and considered to need three men to manage her in rough weather.

The heavy boat had to be physically manhandled into the haven, and in the driving conditions it was impossible for two people to manage this, so Mrs Darling was summoned, in mob-cap and indoor gown, into the cold and wet to try to steady the coble while Grace and her father took an oar each and prepared to bring her out into the wind-tossed sea. Somehow they managed to do this, and despite the entreaties of a distraught Mrs Darling they attempted to pull out towards the wrecked steamship. Whatever her fears Grace pushed them away, knowing with utter clarity what her responsibility was and that come what might she had to fulfil it.

The Northumbrian coble has three seats. She is strongly built and very seaworthy, in length about twenty-one feet and five feet wide amidships. Grace and her father sat side by side on the middle seat, and Grace would have had to pull with remarkable strength to keep up with her father. She wrote later, self-deprecating as always: "I have often had occasion to be in the boat with my father for want of better help, but never at the saving of life before, and I pray God may never be again".

It was impossible to direct the boat against the north wind and the driven sea, and in the vicious conditions William Darling allowed her to be swept southward for half a mile or so. Then somehow or other the two of them brought her round to get some small shelter from the lee of the Blue Caps, now more exposed with the falling tide, but with treacherous rocks below. The conditions remained atrocious, with a bitter wind, a drenching spray, little or no visibility, dangerous currents swirling round the rocks and the sea heaving with an enormous swell.

Meanwhile Mrs Darling, her pleas having failed, climbed the stairway to the lantern and looked out. She could see nothing of the boat, and said that she momentarily passed out. But she looked again, and there at a distance was the coble emerging from the depths of the tidal stream.

A famous picture shows the father and daughter rowing to the rescue. It is not entirely realistic because it shortens the distance between the wreck and the lighthouse, which is actually about three-quarters of a mile in a direct line, but the scene is a very dramatic one. The truth is that William Darling and his daughter sat side by side amidships, each with an oar, and one can imagine the strain Grace was under as she tried to match the strength of her father. The swell was terrific and the sea rolled and twisted below them, with fierce currents around the jagged rocks.

It was necessary to travel a full mile by the route they had to follow, and how they managed to row the rest of the way to reach the near-survivors defies the imagination. William Darling was a strong man, but he was fifty-four years old. Grace, as has been said, was slightly built, and without any great inherent strength. But she was experienced in handling an oar, and sheer determination gave her a near-miraculous sense of purpose, so that after perhaps three-quarters of an hour of terrible toil they managed to reach the rock.

The Rescue

The Big Harker Rock
Having rowed with her father a mile through treacherous seas to the end of this rock, Grace had to handle the boat herself while William Darling was on the reef calming and organising the nine survivors.

But now came Grace's sternest test of all. Nine survivors were revealed on a ledge above the turbulent sea. They were naturally in a state of extreme emotion, and there came a risk that in their urgency they would swamp the coble. So William Darling had to wait until the swell lifted the boat and then jump on to the rock to quieten and organise the bedraggled little group. Meanwhile Grace had to be left on her own in the boat, take both oars and try to keep the coble from being smashed to pieces against the rock. As an old man her father said that the worst moment of his entire life was when he had to leave his cherished daughter to fend for herself, alone in the open boat and in these frightful conditions of wind and sea.

Grace's performance has been recognised as superb seamanship, more fitted to a well-tried mariner than a frail young woman of twenty-two. The scene almost defies the imagination. Grace coped in tidal waters below this treacherous reef under a heavy sky and in a bitter gale, in a wildly tossing sea and with the rain and spray soaking her through and through. For a few moments at least, while her father marshalled the survivors on the rock, she was totally responsible for the lives of all of them. No-one has ever doubted her courage, and no-one could possibly do so. As I have said, it would be unbelievable if we did not know it to be absolutely true.

Grace Darling after the rescue

This is how Grace herself put it:

"I thank God, who enabled me to do so much. I thought it a duty, as no assistance could be had, but still I feel sorry I could do no more".

In writing this she was surely thinking of those on the rock who had already perished: the two young children of the only woman survivor, and an elderly clergyman. The extreme conditions had been too much for them to endure. Three of the crewmen now helped William Darling row the coble back, with Grace ministering to the distraught woman passenger whose two children had died in the bitter cold, and to a badly injured crewman. Grace herself was utterly exhausted, but she did her best to comfort poor Mrs Dawson. The boat was then forced back by two of the crewmen and the superhuman William Darling, to collect the remaining survivors. Back in the lighthouse a much relieved Mrs Darling, so fearful on seeing the coble go out, was treating the survivors to her superb domesticity.

THE AFTERMATH

Now Grace wanted nothing more than to return to her job as assistant lightkeeper, but it was not to be. She was put on a Victorian pedestal, partly from a real appreciation of what she had done, but also for the chance for some people to make themselves rich. Gifts and money were showered upon her, treacly poems were written and recited, and paintings of all descriptions were made; no fuss was too great. Grace accepted all this with her usual politeness, and wrote many letters of appreciation. Some people wanted a lock of hair, and these can be seen in the museum at Bamburgh.

Although her temperament was a courteous one, now and again even her patience was stretched. When one particularly foolish lady wrote saying how thrilled Grace must have been in the high seas, she replied: "You requested me to let you know whether I felt pleasure to be out in a rough sea which I can assure you there is none I think, to any person in their sober senses."

Grace and her father received from the Royal Humane Society special gold medals for gallantry, together with medals from the RNLI, and these were much treasured. Awards were also made to seven young men, including Grace's brother, from the fishing village of North Sunderland, who, on getting a message from the castle lookout about the wreck, and being unable to launch the lifeboat in the raging surf, showed great heroism in rowing for nearly three hours to take a coble out to the lonely rock. By the time they arrived all the survivors had been successfully conveyed to the lighthouse, but the bravery of the fishermen was fully recognised.

Today's harbour at Seahouses

Many other gifts of money, and articles which were of no use, and simply cluttered up the lighthouse, were also received by Grace and politely acknowledged. But she particularly valued a very large bible, and replied: "Kind Sir – I have to acknowledge the receipt of the invaluable present of a most beautiful bible, for which I beg to return my most sincere thanks. May our Almighty Preserver grant all my kind friends with me the sanctified use of that Blessed Volume, at present everything that brings the awful scene to my remembrance leaves a degree of sorrow and regret that it was not in our power to do more – I remain, Sir, your very most obedient humble servant. G H Darling."

One present she was really pleased with was a workbox, and she replied: "The usefulness of such an article can only be judged by people like myself who have had three or four places to search when a little job was to do."

But money she did not want. She said all she needed was five pounds a year, and Grace had no head for money matters.

The media understandingly concentrated on Grace's part in the rescue, and she was concerned that her father was not getting enough recognition. She repeated that William Darling's resolution was as implacable as her own, and that he was in sole command of the operation.

But Grace wrote only reluctantly about the rescue. Her letters are mainly full of family affairs. Thus: "Mother and Father and all are well, but I must leave off as it is getting dark. Mother is knitting stockings for Father..."

She continued to rely on her father for advice, and he was in practical charge of her new life. But his advice was for once misjudged. William Darling felt that on balance the attention to his daughter would be beneficial to her; he said "I should very much like for her to see a little more of the World". Although Grace's own temperament would never have allowed her to rebel against the public's treatment, her father was strong and positive enough to have been well capable of curbing it. But he did not do so, and ultimately it fell to the Duke of Northumberland to appoint himself her guardian, to look after her finances and to vet the many offers of marriage coming her way. But in any case Grace seemed to be apprehensive about marriage; content enough to be tied to a lonely lighthouse she turned away from – as she apparently saw it – subordination to a husband. In her own words, in one of her many letters: "I have not got married yet, for I have heard people say there is luck in leisure". Of course marriage might well have come to her in the fullness of time, but Grace had now very little time left.

The River Coquet at Warksworth
In a vain attempt to cure her ill-health Grace took her first-ever holiday, and walked with her sister Thomasin along the beautiful river below the castle at Warkworth.

"She Went like Snow"

All the ostentatious attention was now seriously affecting her health. She tried riding a horse in the hills, and walked by the river beneath the great castle of Warkworth, but she was finding colds impossible to shake off, though she continued to write optimistic letters. This physical weakness may have played its part in making her vulnerable to the consumption that would rapidly carry her away. She had always made short visits to Bamburgh, where her older sister Thomasin now lived, especially for village festivals and at harvest-time, but now she could not spend any time at all at the lighthouse, and was carried to the mainland to be cared for full-time by Thomasin.

Grace added a sentence to a letter from Thomasin to their parents. Her words are smudged, her writing is unsteady, and her spelling has collapsed. It is the message of a very sick person doing her best to sound hopeful:

"Dear Father and Mother
As I cannot wright you a long letter this time pray God in a little time I will wright a long one.
I am your loving Daughter
Grace H Darling"

But this long letter was never written. About a week later, at the age of twenty-six and only four years after her heroic voyage, Grace died in the arms of her father, in whose company she had tried to do her duty throughout her short life.

It fell to Thomasin, not usually given to beauty of expression, to put together four words not often quoted: "She went like snow".

We need not dwell on the grand funeral, the monument, the stone with lines from Wordsworth's poem in the chapel of Inner Farne.

Let us just say that Grace was a modest, straightforward and very brave young woman doing what she saw as her simple duty to save lives at sea, and it is important to countless people, old and young, that her example should never be forgotten. She has remained my heroine for seventy years, and I am glad to have written her story in these pages.